BIZARRE CARS

BIZARRE CARS

Colin Burnham

OSPREY
AUTOMOTIVE

Published in 1990 by Osprey Publishing
Limited
59 Grosvenor Street
London WIX 9DA

British Library Cataloguing in Publication
Data

Burnham, Colin
  Bizarre Cars
  I. Cars
  I. Title
  629. 222

ISBN 0-85045-991-5

Editor Nicholas Collins
Page Design Angela Posen
Phototypeset by Keyspools Ltd,
Golborne, Lancs
Printed in Hong Kong

About the author

Colin Burnham is a freelance photojournalist whose pictures and stories
have appeared in numerous car magazines in Britain, Europe and North
America. As features editor of Street Machine magazine during the 1980s
Colin reported on all kinds of specialist automotive pursuits and witnessed
some of the most bizarre road-going creations ever conceived. He is the
author of four books, including Air-cooled Volkswagens, Classic
Volkswagens and California Classics (all Osprey Colour Series), and he
drives an all-original 1971 Rover Coupé.

Acknowledgements

The author wishes to thank Street Machine, Britain's leading specialist car
magazine, for permission to reproduce many photographs used in this book,
and the owners and builders of these extraordinary vehicles. He extends
special thanks to Paul Jeffries for the excellence of his research.

Front cover
*Ray Christopher's amazing V8-
powered chopper; one of the most
bizarre 'cars' ever to hit the road*

Title page
*Whoops, sorry mate! It looks like this
Hillman Imp has just been run over by
a steamroller . . . and that is exactly
how its creators wanted it to look!*

Half-title page
*Volkswagen's venerable Beetle has
provided a basis for numerous
cutomising ideas, though none more
bizarre than this!*

Rear cover
*'Claustraphobia' is the world's lowest
Mini. See 'Radical Stuff', page 74*

For a catalogue of all books published by Osprey Automotive
please write to:

**The Marketing Manager, Consumer Catalogue Department
Osprey Publishing Ltd, 59 Grosvenor Street, London, W I X 9DA**

Contents

What better form of advertising for a shoe repair store in car-crazy Los Angeles? The custom-made fibreglass boot is attached to a VW Beetle chassis, and the vehicle is driven daily

Street Machines

The street machine movement encompasses innumerable kinds of modified cars. These road-going machines mean more to their owners than the tin boxes driven by 'Joe Motorist'. Street machines take many months, and sometimes years, of meticulous building. The result is always something highly individual and a light year away from anything available in a surburban car showroom.

In the process of building the car of the owner's dreams engines are swapped, suspension and transmissions improved, and the bodywork is radically modified. Theoretically, nothing limits the final result except the creator's imagination and the depth of his or her finances.

Any source can serve as an inspiration, but the majority are drawn to the traditions of American customising. The nostalgic 1950s hot rod, the chopped and lowered 'Leadsled' have their place, but increasingly the 'Pro Street' machine that looks as if it has just finished a stint on the drag strip is gaining ground.

Some cars never achieve anything more radical than a wild paint job, but others take such extreme routes that it is hard to identify what car, if any, originally left the factory.

But whatever the car, whatever the style, the result is the same; the vehicle is there to be driven. And the rewards for all the hard work, money spent and frustration are pride of ownership and the admiring, even envious glances the driver enjoys when his or her dream machine eventually hits the streets.

Right
A superb example of the in-vogue 'Pro Street' style, this Ford Zephyr Mk II owned by Nick Kemp, boasts dragster engineering while masquerading as a road car. Under the louvred bonnet is a fully tuned 7-litre American V8 engine which produces in excess of 550 bhp. The chopped roof and monster-sized rear tyres squeezed inside the original wheelarches make this old Ford one of the meanest looking street machines in Britain

Above

This Morris Minor is not the kind of car that midwives used to drive! Owned by Gary Ellis, the convertible Minor has been modified several times since he bought it secondhand in 1967. He fitted many types of engine and wheels and painted the car in various different colours over the years before undertaking a complete rebuild in the mid-1980s to produce a real 'state of the art' chopped convertible Minor. Now the Porsche Red hot rod boasts a highly modified 3.9-litre Rover V8 engine and is fitted with racing style suspension and ventilated disc brakes plus Halibrand racing alloy wheels to cope with the performance from its 350 bhp engine – over ten times the output of the original A-series unit

Below

*Back to the 1950s – a time when customised cars were called 'kustomised kars'
and those that were drastically chopped and lowered were known as 'Leadsleds',
so called because of the heavyweight lead filler used to create their smooth
flowing lines. But with the nostalgia boom of the 1980s, the Leadsleds are still
cruising the streets in both America and England. Owned by Bruce Gill, this 1949
Mercury, a traditional favourite for the Leadsled treatment, was built in America
by one of the original 'kustomisers', Gene Winfield, in the 1980s. It sports a very
up-to-date 350 ci Chevrolet engine, but it still has the traditional accoutrements
of whitewall tyres, side 'lake' pipes and a pair of 'Appleton' spotlights*

Above
Another throwback to the times when the guys and gals cruised Main Street in chopped and lowered 'sleds'. Over 30 years later, Lee McDouall glides the street of Hatfield, Hertfordshire in his 1950s-style kustomised Morris Minor. Too Kool!

Left and below
Owner Andy Saunders based this unique 'Leadsled' on a 1968 Volvo 121 when he was just 19 years old. He removed the roof and made the Swedish tank a convertible before smoothing-out the bodywork and transforming the car into a garishly authentic-looking example of 1950s-style US customising. As if there is any doubt about the car's period inspiration there is a rock 'n' roll diner scene embroidered into the upholstery just for confirmation

Shoulder-to-shoulder with the 1950s custom car enthusiasts are the street rodders. They believe in 'having fun with old cars'. Early Ford products, especially the Model T and Model B 'Deuce Coupe' have always been the favourite starting points for street rods in America, but in Britain it is the good old Ford Popular. Alan Humphrey's 1953 Pop features a supercharged Ford Mustang V8, Jaguar independent rear suspension (IRS) and tube front axle. Look's fun, eh

Above
A still from the movie American Graffiti? No, this is an absolutely faithful replica of the famous 'Deuce Coupe' hot rod, bonnetless and fenderless, like the one driven by John Milner in the film. It was photographed in Milwaukee

Right
Rock band, ZZ Top, are almost as famous for the wild cars they use in their videos as they are for their music. For example, the bright red 1933 Ford Coupe with the striking 'ZZ' graphics that starred in their Eliminator video. This is a similar rendition based on a 1933 Plymouth coupe and it has a 3.5-litre Rover V8 engine and Jaguar suspension

Left
This is what is known as a radical T-bucket — 5.3-litres, 12 cylinders in 'V' formation, six fully-chromed carburettors and no problem checking the oil!

Right
You would not guess that somewhere beneath that bulbous bodywork is a Triumph TR7

Below
Nothing is sacred in the world of street machines, not even that which is ranked by many as the most beautiful sportscar ever: the Jaguar E-Type. This 'Pro Street Cat' runs a 427 ci Chevrolet 'Rat' engine along with a set of tyres and rims that provide somewhat better traction than the originals

Above
It looks as if it might have come from the factory like this. Some relatively subtle modifications have turned Richard Haskell's 1970 Jaguar XJ6 into a one-off coupé. And just look at the size of the boot – plenty of room for the golf clubs!

Above
*A roof-chop and a good paint job can
turn an average looking car into a real
head turner. This nicely chopped Ford
Granada came all the way from
Holland to take part in* Street
Machine *magazine's John O' Groats to
Land's End 'Cruise for Charity' in 1987*

Left
The car that used to be known affectionally as the 'Anglebox'. the Ford Anglia has long been popular with the custom fraternity and this 1967 example has received the full works. In addition to chopping the roof and fitting a Jaguar IRS, owner Gary Layton has somehow managed to shoehorn a Rover V8 into the engine bay. And if that was not enough, it's supercharged too

Above
Another popular car, but chop the roof, sort out the bodywork, add an American V8 engine and you've got one hot Capri that is guaranteed to turn heads in every High Street

Left

How's this for access? There's no need to crawl underneath for repairs on this Mini – just flip up the whole body and work in comfort. Built by Neil Fenn, the car is now rear wheel drive with a Ford Corsair axle at the rear and Triumph Herald suspension at the front. Power comes from a 2-litre V4 Corsair engine

Right

You would certainly do a 'double take' if you saw this Mini in your rear-view mirror. Thanks to the attentions of a Midlands bodywork firm this little pick-up acquired an extra pair of wheels at the back and a Mercedes-Benz radiator grille, plus headlights, at the front – now it's a real upmarket Mini

Above

This 1955 Peugeot 203 has been rebuilt in the style of a 'Lowrider'. 'Lowriders' emerged from the Chicano ghettos of Los Angeles, California. Here, sons of Mexican immigrants, who had come to work in the broiling heat of the fields, fitted old Chevys and similar makes with hydraulic suspension systems which could alter ride-height at the flick of a switch. Drivers can even make their cars 'jump' as they cruise along. Chris Adam's Peugeot has no less than four extra car batteries fitted in the boot to provide power for the hydraulics

Above
Lift the boot lid of this Stateside
Lincoln Continental and, boy, what an
impressive set-up!

Left
The interior of this early 1960s
Consul-Capri, luxuriously upholstered
in deep buttoned crushed velvet and
sporting a chromed chain-link
steering wheel, is typical of the
flambouyant 'Lowrider' style

Left
'Bullitt' was a film that featured a
Mustang fastback in its famous car
chase sequence. This 'stang pays
tribute to the legend in its bonnet
murals inspired by the movie, which
starred Steve McQueen

Above
When a Ford V8 Mustang engine is
this clean it is almost a shame to start
it up . . .

Right
But here is proof that Alan Revell's show-stopper does see action. This super-clean street machine represents an intense labour of love on the part of the owner. He lives in Essex and collects trophies like they are going out of fashion

Right
This is the side of the Mustang that most onlookers never see. Nevertheless, every component beneath the car is either chrome-plated, polished or painted to the same exacting standard as the exterior

Monster Motored

Anything from a typical family banger to a miniscule bubble car is fair game for monster motor treatment. These vehicles were never designed to carry such phenomenal horsepower. Half their attraction lies in marrying mammoth, highly tuned, supercharged, turbocharged or fuel-injected big block engines with innocuous-looking bodies.

Occasionally, even the most evolved automotive 'lump' is not enough for builders chasing the Grail of ultimate performance, so an aircraft engine is pressed into service. If it was ever possible to press 'the pedal to the metal' in anger then the speed off the line would be almost explosive. The only place to find out just what a monster motor is capable of is on a drag strip, if you are brave enough.

Back in the 1950s and 1960s, bubble cars were all the rage despite having just three wheels, a motorcycle engine and a single door at the front. But they were nothing like this one. Based on an Isetta, this little bundle of trouble has got a Porsche engine stuffed in the back plus some rather meaty looking wheels and tyres. Now, without those wheelie bars just behind the rear wheels, too much power and you'd be quickly doing a back flip – and the bubble would burst!

Below
A standard condition Vauxhall Cresta PA can do 0–60 mph in just over 16 seconds.
That sounds quite fast for an early 1960s car until you consider that this high-
riding example, fitted with a V12 Jaguar engine, can accelerate three times as
quickly: it can be travelling at 60 mph in a touch over five seconds!

Above
The Jaguar engine has twice as many cylinders and almost double the cubic capacity of the original Vauxhall unit. Owner, Chris Meek, had to build a special chassis and fit Jaguar independent rear suspension, Transit van front suspension and two Transit steering columns welded together to steer the flip-fronted freak

You would certainly cause a stir if you arrived at Harrods or The Ritz in this machine! Built by John Dodd and appropriately named 'The Beast', this car has to be the ultimate street machine with an engine capacity equal to that of 27 Minis! Underneath that 18 ft long, custom-built body complete with pukka Rolls-Royce grille and golden flying lady, is a 27-litre V12 Rolls-Royce Merlin aircraft engine which can take the car up to 150 miles per hour – and probably more if only someone could find a road long enough!

Left
Apart from the slightly over-sized wheels and tyres, Gordon Jones' ex-Post Office van looks quite ordinary, but crammed under the bonnet is a massive Chevrolet V8 engine with a capacity of more than 5-litres

Above
The Mini's new muscle plant needs two fans to keep it cool in commuter traffic

Above
They said it could not be done, but Ian Hewings proved them wrong by shoe-horning a Lotus twin-cam engine sideways into his Mini. Needless to say, mating the engine to the Mini Traveller gearbox involved more than a few hours work, but 0–60 mph in 7 seconds and a terminal speed of 130 mph no doubt makes the effort all worthwhile

Right
Fiat 500? Try Fiat 3500! Owner, Bob Preston, has transformed this rear engined micro-car into a front-engined mini-monster with a Rover V8, Jaguar 'S' Type rear axle and massive rear tyres. There is now so little room inside that Bob has to drive from the back seat and flip-up the whole body to perform routine engine checks

Left

This old Renault Dauphine used to have a puny 845cc engine mounted out back. Now it has a Cadillac V8 engine of nearly eight times the size fitted up front – well, nearer the front anyway. The Caddy 'lump' is so big that the driver now has to sit in the back seat to steer the car – hence the car's nickname, 'Back Seat Driver'

Overleaf

Stuart Vallance's hard-charging 1962 Mk II Consul (as featured on the front cover of the first issue of Street Machine) *is fitted with a supercharged Chevrolet 'Rat' engine that is over four times the size of the original. The performance is earth-shattering. 'Henry Hirise' can reach 60 mph from a standing-start in a little over four seconds and 100 mph takes not much more than ten!*

What a motor! The highly tuned, supercharged and seriously chromed Chevrolet engine will propel this American Capri through the quarter-mile barrier in a shade over 10 seconds on road tyres

Above
*Wide rear tyres are tucked under
standard Capri wheelarches in
contemporary Pro Street style*

Below
*The 'race car' look for Britain's
favourite family saloon. With massive
aluminium 'wheeltubs' in place of the
rear seat, aluminium panelling
throughout and a huge 4.6-litre Chevy
engine, there is certainly no room for
the kids in this Escort*

4a Above and right
This Ford Sierra is unlike any other company hack you might see being thrashed up and down the outside lane of a motorway. For a start, the massive rear wheel tubs and roll cage means there's no room in the back to hang a suit jacket and, worse still, the huge 8.2-litre tuned Chrysler V8 engine is so thirsty that the car probably would not make it to the next service station. But that does not worry owner, Geoff Hauser, because he built the car especially for the drag strip where it can reach a speed of 157 miles per hour in less than 9 seconds

Above
As if 7.5-litres of American V8 engine were not enough, Rick Dobbertin's Chevy Nova has twin turbochargers, a supercharger and nitrous oxide injection to give him just that little bit of extra 'go' when he regularly exercises the machine on public roads

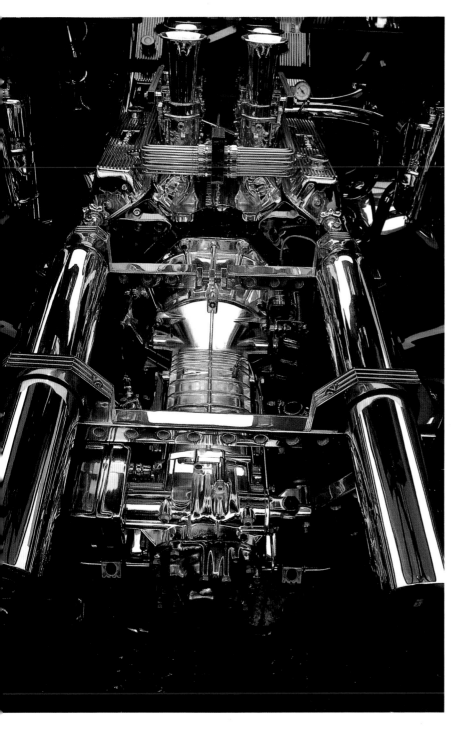

If all that glitters is not gold then De Tomaso Pantera owner George Peloquin of California has wasted a lot of time and money on a fool's mission. 'Pur Gold', as the car's licence plate reads, is a £100,000 street machine that features what has been described as a 'million dollar' driveline. And yes, it is all genuine 24 karat gold plate!

Different Strokes . . .

Customising is essentially expressing individuality by transforming a factory production vehicle until it fits the owner's idea of automotive perfection. Often it is just the maufacturer's choice of engine size that seems wrong, or the 'as-supplied' style of wheels and tyres that do not match the driver's expectations. But sometimes, something more fundamental is 'wrong', so bodywork, interior and paint job are entirely re-styled to reveal that 'personal touch'.

Times change along with styles and beauty is, after all, in the eyes of the customiser. It really is a matter of individual taste. What is more, it might be said that the people who created the vehicles in this chapter are just a shade more 'individual' than most . . .

Left
Customising, as a means of self-expression, can give as much pleasure to onlookers as to the creator. Who would not smile at this Austin Cambridge, with its custom-made 'Continental kit' and 'quad' tail-lights?

Left
Escort lovers will perhaps recognise
the basis for this extraordinary car.
All other are excused their bafflement

Above
'Six wheels on my wagon (and a
skeleton in the back)' goes the old
song. The owner of this somewhat
macabre Escort calls it 'Soul Streaker'

Above
Not all Cortina Mk I versions receive the rear end jack-up treatment . . .

Right
Exhuberant graphic design and Metalflake paintwork make sure this Cortina Mk IV gets noticed!

Left
You would never lose this Cortina Mk II in a car park, that's for sure!

Left
With flamed paintwork more akin to
1950s hot rods and a huge tail fin
reminiscent of the 1960s Plymouth
Road Runner, Geoff Rozenberg's
Cortina Mk III seems to have
something of an identity crisis

Above
'Joust Looking' is a 1972 Triumph TR6
with murals based on the Saint George
and the Dragon theme – a slightly
eccentric paint job, even if it is a
British sportscar

Left
Vette Dream? The All-American
Chevrolet Corvette sportscar in, er,
non-factory colours . . .

Above
This 'murialled' Ford Fiesta was
Custom Car *magazine's idea of fun*
back in the 1970s

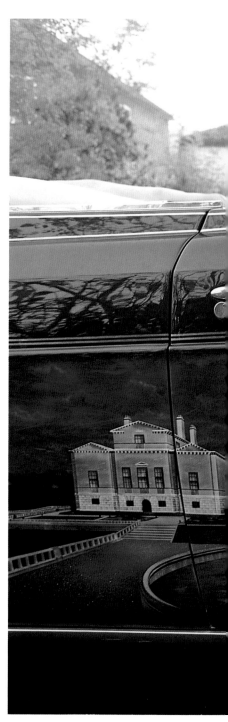

Decorum holds no bounds for the customiser as is proven by these Rolls-Royce motorcars with their exquisitely detailed murals. At least the subject matter for the paintings is consistent with the marque's image

Left
Reliant Robin as 'Knight Rider'? One assumes someone had a sense of humour

Above
Words fail when trying to describe this somewhat disguised Volkswagen, suffice it to say, it is a regular attraction at VW events in sunny Southern California

For would-be movie star Dennis Woodruff, the road to fame and fortune is travelled in a Lincoln Continental during daily drives around Hollywood. The car is literally covered in self-promotional material. Woodruff says he wants to become a legend of the silver screen in the James Dean mould. He has taped hundreds of photographs of himself to the vehicle and added banners that bear the message 'Actor seeks big break in movie'. And all this effort was not in vain. Phil Collins hired Woodruff to play the part of his chauffeur in a pop video. Pity the rock star could not have used the mobile billboard as well

Every year a group of Manhattan Beach, Los Angeles residents get together to create a 'theme car'. The chosen subject in 1989 was 'the beach' and this unlikely looking Pontiac station wagon was the victim. Wacky

Left

Japri or Capriguar? Trevor Wright's unusual amalgamation is part Ford Capri and part Jaguar XJ6, but whatever you call it, it is certainly 'different' . . .

Overleaf

And so to bed, leastways that is often the case for Mo Reynolds' 1968 Ford Torino. A plumber and dedicated frequenter of night clubs from Lincoln, Mo has been exhibiting this car at Street Machine magazine events for longer than many care to remember. The car's interior, which has just the hint of an Indian restaurant about its decor, also suggests a 'Sleeping Beauty' fantasy. Indeed, many refer to their car as 'She', but this is ridiculous!

PRIDE & PASSION
1978 to 1987

MODEL
American Ford Torino GT (1968)
owner Mo Reynolds

ENGINE
V8 - 302a - 4,750cc.
23 mpg Drives at 60-65 mph.
Mechanic Brian Berry.

EXTERIOR
Paint done by Pete Carter, in Kelly green Gloss,
Chrome and vinyl. Chrome & trims, Chroming done by Pro's Cast.
7-14 8 spoke Rocket wheels with pro-trac F70-14s.

INTERIOR
Gold & red velour, Engine turned, Home made dashboard & console.
Roof lining done in velour blend & towers, all ornament work
done by Pro-Fabri-Craft, and all carpets and done by Little Richard.

This car is used on the road and does
approximately 8000 to 10000 miles per year.
This display remembers Neil Jarrett, Wentworths, Jasper Road.
Not a lot of money.

PRIDE & PASSION
1988
OWNER FROM
Mo Reynolds LINCOLN

NEW METALWORK
In March 1987 this car was taken to Kenny
Burkills at Doncaster to have new metal put in the
arches, floor pan, doors and in the wings.
This was because of a rusty problem.
It has also been fitted with a new
twin exhaust system

NEW PAINT
The car was resprayed to match the
bonnet, boot & roof also new graphics were
added. The paint on both sides of the car was
taken back to metal before it was repainted.
14 months on it was back on the road again.
This car has been on the custom car scene since
1978

DETAILS ON GRAPHICS
Highlights on the graphics was
done by Castle Customs of Lincoln.

EJU 577K

Radical Stuff

With the emphasis one hundred per cent on fun and frivolity, some cars have been almost totally re-designed, their bodywork so drastically modified that it might be difficult to decide what make of car it was originally, or even establish front from back! Their creators are masters of metalwork with a bent for producing the longest, lowest, shortest contraption possible, or something just a wee bit 'out of the ordinary'. Some of these master works include a 'steamrollered' Hillman Imp, a really mini Mini and a Pontiac which does not seem to know which way it's going. These are the cars that have been wildy stretched, extremely shortened, thoroughly squashed, chopped, channelled, iced, diced and spliced – and they are all absolutely wild!

Right
Standing at a mere 26.5 in high, Perry Watkins and Danny Curtis's radical Hillman Imp holds the Guinness record for the World's Lowest Car. It's also road taxed and MOT tested, officer!

Here is another of Andy Saunders' madcap creations – the world's lowest Mini. 'Claustrophobia' as the Mini is called, is a former Guinness world record holder and is fully road legal. With its roof-line about the same height as a normal Mini bonnet, people just cannot believe their eyes when the Mini drives down the street. One lady thought it must have been built specially for a midget – until 6 ft 4 in Andy crawled out!

Below
*At the 1987 Motorvation show staged
by* Street Machine *magazine, well
known BBC TV presenter, Bill Giles,
was filmed giving a weather report
from the driving seat of the Mini*

Above
*All roads are open to the driver of a
car that is just 34.5 in high!*

It's that man Saunders again – he just won't leave Minis alone! This 1964 example has been shortened by 31 in, and with a twin-carburettor 1300 cc engine it can even pull wheelies in reverse. Andy says his 'Mini Ha Ha', as it is named, is frightening to drive but great for parking

Left

There may not be much surf around but these guys were certainly having fun looking for it in their drastically shortened, open-top Mini

Right and overleaf

This is what happens when you take 18 in from the centre of a Volkswagen – you end up with a 'Thinbug'! After owning four relatively standard Beetles, Californian engineering student, Andrew Hancock, thought that it was time he drove something different. This bizarre Bug took many thousands of hours to build but actually cost less than $1000 to complete. Side-on, it appears that there is nothing special about this 1969 VW, but then if you happen to catch sight of it in your rear-view mirror . . .

Above
This used to be a 1975 VW Passat estate . . . and it's certainly in-a-state now!

Right
This one causes a stir in the office car park! Owned by Belgian magazine publisher, Patrice De Bruyne, the American Oldsmobile has been radically chopped and shortened and flame painted the traditional hot rod way

XE-CUTE-R
1964 VOLKSWAGEN
ALL METAL BODY
PORSCHE 911S ENGINE

Owner ED HAPAC
WALNUT CREEK,
CALIFORNIA U.S.A.

Voted most beautiful car in the U.S.A
★ AWARDS

TOP CUSTOM U.S.A
GROUP PROMOTION (GRAND FINALE) LAS VEGAS
STONACKER AWARD, OAKLAND ROADSTER SHOW
SAM BARRISER AWARD, SACRAMENTO AUTORAMA

Left
Owned by Ed Papac from California, this much modified 1964 Beetle named 'XE-CUTE-R' was once voted 'Top Custom in the USA'. It has an all-metal body, a custom-built tubular chassis and is fitted with a 911 Porsche engine. With its eye-catching graphic paint job it's customising 'par excellence'

Above
Originally customised in Sweden by Bernt Carlsson, but now a regular contender on the California show circuit, this 1955 VW Beetle 'Lowrider' (pictured on Britain's M6 at Birmingham) has certainly come a long way from its place of manufacture. What the late Dr Ferdinand Porsche, father of the original Beetle, would have said about the car's chopped roof, wild Metalflake paint job and hydraulic suspension is anyone's guess

Overleaf
A stretched four-door Beetle is just the job for taking those California girls to the beach . . . or to 'Angelo's', a popular haunt for California's Orange County hot rodders

Left

Ultra Limousines' 48 ft stetched 1967 Cadillac is undoubtedly the world's longest limo. It boasts 10 wheels, accommodation for 22 passengers and a 12 ft, 700 gallon pool beneath its boot lid. Only in California . . .

Above
One beer too many? No, you are not seeing things – the Pontiac's body has been mounted back-to-front on its chassis and judging by the parachute at the 'back' there is a pretty powerful engine under the bonnet . . . or should that be the boot?

Right
Powered by a 427 ci Chevrolet V8 engine, this 1968 Chevrolet Biscayne has had its boot stretched by several feet which helps it to pull even better wheelies!

Overleaf
It has two bonnets, two front seats and even two steering wheels. But to end any confusion about which way this 1940 Dodge is meant to go, there are number plates at either end which read respectively 'Coming' and 'Going'

So Bizarre!

There are some cars in the world of customising which to the onlooker suggest that the creator must have taken complete leave of his senses or perhaps indulged in several glasses of brewed beverage too many before starting work. These are the cars of pure fantasy, where their builder has given full rein to his sometimes surreal imagination. Who could conceive the idea of making a road-going helicopter or a street-legal speedboat? And what kind of person puts a big V8 engine in a milkfloat, or makes a JCB digger into a dragster?

The ideas for these zany creations can come from space-age vehiculer fantasies such as Dr. Who's Dalek to more individual creations like Andy Saunders' somewhat 'cosmic' Citroen. And while some are built purely for show, others have been designed from the beginning to be street-legal, their owners delighting in the shock value of their unique machines. Wild, weird or wonderful, these cars illustrate the truly bizarre side of customising.

Ron Heitman's unique contribution to Stateside street culture used to hang 30 ft in the air above an amusement park before this Ohio resident turned the fantasy 'Rocket' into a road-going reality. The front-wheel-drive V8 Oldmobile-powered projectile is capable of 130 mph

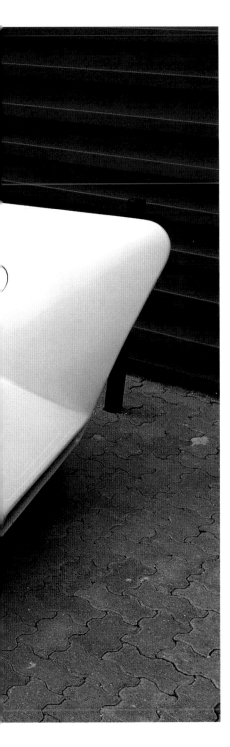

Above
The interior of the Citroen looks more like that of a spaceship with its distinctive upholstery and aeroplane-type steering wheel

Left
This wild looking creation looks like something out of 'Thunderbirds' or maybe even 'Batman', but in fact came from the warped imagination of customiser extraordinaire, Andy Saunders. Who would believe that underneath all that space-age style bodywork is an unassuming 1976 Citroen Pallas CX2200?

Overleaf
Is it a car? Is it a plane? Well, both really. 'G-Whizz' is Bill Carter's off-the-wall Earth-bound Jaguar V12-powered jet car. OK, it cannot fly, but it is fully street-legal

Above

Here is one cement mixer that will not hold up the traffic. Ray Christopher's weird looking cement mixer called 'C-Men-T' has two fully-chromed independent Jaguar rear ends and is powered by a Rover V8 engine

Right

Also conceived by top British show car builder, Ray Christopher, this crazy helicopter was brought down to earth and made right for the road. With front suspension and brakes provided by a Ford Transit van and a Jaguar XJ6, plus power courtesy of a huge Buick V8 with twin-superchargers, Ray's chopper could be quicker on the ground than it was in the air!

Comedian Frank Carson was not serious when he joked about 'Paddy' buying a new sports car – a JCB GT digger – but manufacturers JCB were when they built just that. Though it looks like any other digger, the JCB GT has a 1000 bhp supercharged Chevrolet V8 engine along with special tyres and aeroplane 'jockey' wheels. It can pull wheelies and do over 100 mph!

Left
'Shiver me timbers, 'tis a boat on wheels!' Probably the craziest of all Andy Saunders' concoctions is this 14 ft speedboat with Reliant Regal three-wheeler running gear

Above
Now this really is out of this world – a Dalek from the Doctor Who TV series spotted at Sandown Park Racecourse in Surrey. The doctor behind this Dalek is Perry Watkins who modelled his creation on an Emporer Dalek from the TV series starring John Pertwee. Perry's Dalek is powered by an Austin 1100 engine and rides on two Mini sub-frames. There is just enough room for two people inside. But anybody who gets too close is warned: 'We will exterminate' – which blasts through a 30 watt speaker

This unusual looking milk float has certainly got a 'lotta bottle' under the throttle! With a Chevrolet V8 engine and a top speed of 120 mph, Ray Christopher's 1955 Manulectric float could do the rounds in double quick time — but probably not very quietly!

'Sonic', a unique twin-Rover V8 engined six-wheeler, adds a whole new dimension to the expession 'wind in the hair' motoring. Built for wheel manufacturers, Wolfrace, this amazing looking projectile has separate driver and passenger compartments, computer control and hoards of electronic gadgetry, plus steering on all four front wheels and a top speed approaching 170 miles per hour. Barry Treacy, the man who inspired 'Sonic's' construction also sponsored the Wolfrace wheels on Richard Noble's World Land Speed Record machine – Thrust II

Above
*The alternative cool cruiser – a
motorcycle powered freezer!*

SHIT HOT

Commercial Customs

Commercial vehicles were, and are, designed for vital but utilitarian tasks. Any concept of luxury is absent from the vocabulary of engineers obsessed with achieving 'maximum cube' load volumes, or optimising the ergonomics of delivery vans in urban areas.

Put these same vehicles in the customising world and something miraculous happens. The carpenter's runaround suddenly sports V8 muscle, the sides of a mundane panel van are immediately turned into a canvas for a science fiction fantasy landscape, and a maximum-rated tractor unit becomes an ideal host for a jet engine.

And with all the space in the rear of both trucks and vans, custom builders have vied to surpass each other with ever more luxurious and ingenious interiors. Drinks cabinets, television and video, full sound systems, aquaria and even one-armed bandits seem almost common-place in the archetypical 'passion wagon'.

Left
Andy Saunders has dubbed his 24 ft, six-wheel creation 'Asorta Transporta', which is just as good a way as any to describe this unique Citroen CX-based behemoth

Above
You can see it now, both chromed
stacks blowing smoke as this All-
American rig heads on out down Route
128 towards its drop in Chicago three
days away. Despite the wallop of its
Rover V8 engine, the origins of this
'truck' are closer to Luton airport. A
Bedford CF van donated the basics for
this one-of-a-kind

Right
In the beginning there was 'Big Foot',
then came 'Bear Foot' and a host of
metal-munching four-wheel-drive
monster trucks. But brothers Chris
and Phil Griffiths definitely scored a
first with 'Club Foot'; a custom-built
4WD Mini pickup with Rover SD1 V8
power

This cartoon-like novelty is appropriately named 'Abbreviation'. It began life as a 1976 Bedford CF delivery van. Room is rather scarce – the whole vehicle is 10 in shorter than a standard Mini

Right
No Kalashnikovs in the back of this Afghan-look truck. It is pictured closer to home at an indoor event in Manchester

Below right
Ray Christopher's show car transporter takes the form of a scaled-down Peterbilt truck – what better?

Below
Steve Murty's truck never fails to be a show-stopper. The sight of this yellow monster pulling hundred yard wheelies while continuously belching flame from its twin stacks is just something-else!

Overleaf
How about this for speedy deliveries? Steve Murty's Ford Cargo truck is fitted with a Rolls-Royce Avon jet engine. This aeroplane propulsion unit develops no less than 24,000 bhp and nearly has the truck airborne at over 200 mph

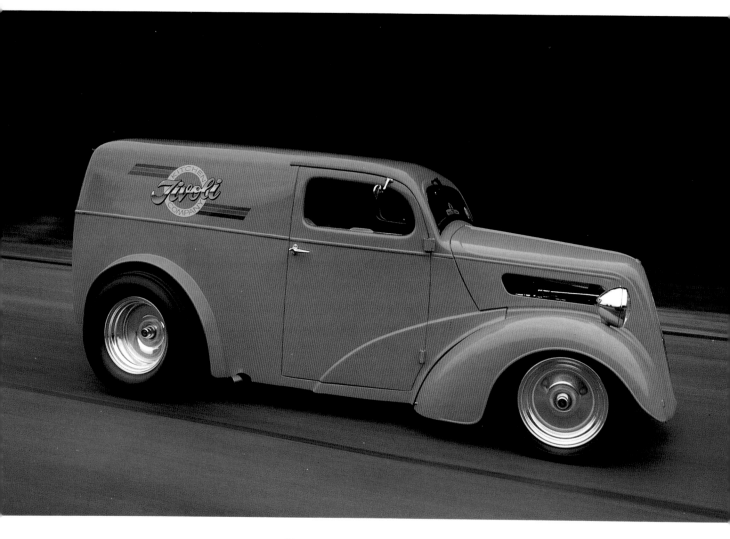

Above
*This old Ford van is not quite the
average company delivery mule. With
its chopped roof, Jaguar rear
suspension, and supercharged 5-litre
Mustang engine in place of the
original four-cylinder side-valve unit,
Keith Atkinson's Fordson makes those
routine errands seem less of a chore*

Right
*For human beings beer and cars never
go together but this Bass Worthington
special brew is a fine piece of product
advertising*

Up, up and away — another crushing victory for 'Sky High'. The mammoth 4WD Ford Transit is powered by a 7.5-litre Ford V8 engine and with its specially made heavy-duty chassis, gargantuan earthmover tyres plus roll-over cage, 'Sky High' weighs-in at about seven tons. With driving like that the owner must pay one heck of an insurance premium!

Above
Is it just a nice paint job, or a work of art? Many hours of demanding labour and mind-stretching attention to detail have gone into Ian Beddoe's Toyota van

Right
It is hard to believe that this lounge area was once reserved for heavy packing cases and car spares